From Seed

by Ruth Mattison

Pioneer Valley Educational Press, Inc.

Here is an **apple**.

Apples are good for you.
Where do we get apples from?

Can you see the **seeds**
in the apple?
Apple seeds are little and brown.

The apple seed is **planted**
in the ground.
The seed grows.
It grows and grows.
It grows into an apple tree.

Look at the **blossom**.

Look at the **insect**.

Insects carry **pollen** from blossom to blossom.

This is called **pollination**.

The apples will grow after the insects bring the pollen to the blossoms.
The apples grow and grow and grow.

It is time to pick the apples!

From Seed to Apple

apple

blossom

insect

planted

pollen

pollination

seeds